COLUMBIA UNIVERSITY
DEPARTMENT OF SLAVIC LANGUAGES

SLAVIC STUDIES
Slavic Bibliography Series

CZECH AND SLOVAK LITERATURE

by

William E. Harkins

Instructor in Slavic Languages

Klement Šimončič

Lecturer in Slovak

With a Bibliography on Lusatian Literature

by

Clarence A. Manning

Assistant Professor of Slavic Languages

ACKNOWLEDGEMENT

The preparation and publication of the several series of works under SLAVIC STUDIES have been made possible by a grant from the Rockefeller Foundation to the Department of Slavic Languages of Columbia University.

Ernest J. Simmons
Executive Officer

PREFATORY NOTE

This pamphlet is one of a series of bibliographies on Slavic literature, language and oral tradition, designed to serve
the needs of scholars and students in these fields, as well as
for use by libraries seeking to create or supplement collections in Slavic studies.

The present bibliography is not exhaustive. It is an attempt to select those works dealing with Czech and Slovak literature and related subjects which are important for a comprehensive knowledge of this field as a whole. While some prefer-
ence has been given to works in English and other Western
European languages, no such work has been included unless it
was itself of substantial worth. The great majority of the
titles are Czech or Slovak.

Since a certain knowledge of history, cultural development,
philology and the history of the literary language is essential
for a proper understanding of literature, such works have by
no means been excluded. A more extensive bibliography of works
on Czechoslovak philological and linguistic problems will be
found in the Department's bibliography on Slavic philology in
this series. A similar all-Slavic bibliography exists for literature of oral tradition, and for this reason Czech and Slovak
oral literature have been excluded here, though works treating
the interpenetration of folk and written literatures have been
included.

As a rule, magazine articles have been listed only when
they fill important lacunae in literary history or criticism.
This has been done partly because of the lesser permanence and
more specialized nature of many articles, partly because of
the rarity of Czechoslovak periodicals in the United States.
Lists of Czech and Slovak periodicals dealing with literary
science or criticism have, however, been appended.

The bibliography is arranged chronologically. The division
into periods is not entirely orthodox, but has been adapted to
suit the needs of the subject matter of the entries themselves.
More refined categorization would have made the task of grouping certain books difficult; thus it would seem to be impossible to separate the period of the Czech Enlightenment from

that of Pre-Romanticism, desirable as this might be, for many works treat both subjects, and writers of the period (Jungmann, for example) underwent both influences.

Anthologies have been included, since they are often hard to find without bibliographical references. Where the title leaves any doubt as to the contents, they have been designated as such.

It will be obvious that no single library in the United States contains all the works included in this bibliography, and, indeed, only in New York can a substantial majority of them be found. Still, it will be desirable to list certain of the more important collections of Czech and Slovak publications:

Library of Congress, Washington, D.C.
New York Public Library, New York, N.Y.
Webster Branch, New York Public Library, New York, N.Y.
Columbia University Library, New York, N.Y.
Harvard University Library, Cambridge, Mass.
Yale University Library, New Haven, Conn.
Cleveland Public Library, Cleveland, Ohio.
Toman Branch, Chicago Public Library, Chicago, Ill.
University of Texas Library, Austin, Texas.
University of Minnesota Library, Minneapolis, Minn.
Hoover Library, Stanford University, Palo Alto, Cal.
University of Colorado Library, Boulder, Colo.
University of Pennsylvania Library, Philadelphia, Pa.
University of Princeton Library, Princeton, N.J.
St. Procopius College Library, Lisle, Ill. (Czech).
Osterhaut Free Library, Wilkes-Barre, Pa. (Slovak).

Grateful acknowledgment is made to Professors René Wellek, Otakar Odložilík, Ernest J. Simmons and Ad. Stender-Petersen and to others for valuable advice concerning the form and contents of this bibliography.

W. E. Harkins

C O N T E N T S

CZECH LITERATURE

AND

RELATED FIELDS

by

William E. Harkins

BIBLIOGRAPHY ON CZECH LITERATURE

INTRODUCTION

Literature has been written on Czechoslovak soil since the second half of the ninth century, and thus Czechoslovak literature is, in a sense, the eldest of its Slavic brothers. With the coming of Christianity to Moravia there was created a literature in Old Church Slavonic, a literary language close to the Moravian vernacular of the day, together with an ideological tradition which emphasized the equal right of every people to worship God in its own tongue and to possess a national culture of its own. The several texts which have survived from this period or the one following it are presumably a mere fragment of a much more extensive literary production.

Though the Great Moravian Empire had close cultural and, perhaps, political ties with the East and Byzantium during the latter part of the ninth century, Bohemia and Moravia could not remain indifferent to the stronger German state which arose to the West, and, after a period of vaccilation between pro-Eastern and pro-Western tendencies, these lands were finally incorporated into the Holy Roman Empire, while Slovakia fell to Hungary. In certain periods the Czech princes were successful in obtaining a large degree of political and cultural autonomy for their lands. Though Latin largely replaced Church Slavonic as the literary language, the latter did not entirely disappear, and Slavonic religious literature continued to be written in the monasteries of Sázava and later Na Slovanech. A small number of hymns attest to the growing claim of the vernacular tongue to a literature of its own.

Only with the end of the thirteenth century did the secular ideology of chivalry and the increasing wealth and leisure of the nobility and townspeople create the premises for a great literature in Czech. The fourteenth century is perhaps the "Golden Age" of Bohemia, a period when Czech literary art, architecture and painting were on a level comparable with the best in Western Europe. In the genres of the chivalric epic, lyric song, satire, medieval mystery play, sermon, religious legend and prose dialogue, the Czechs succeeded in creating native forms and a native style, often showing the strong influence of national proverbs, folk tales and folk expressions,

1

even when the original subject was borrowed. Czech writers also succeeded in imprinting a strong stamp of national ideology on borrowed material. The vernacular language was developed to such an extent that during the 1360's a Latin-Czech dictionary of theological and scholarly terms was compiled, containing about 7,000 entries, the first such attempt in Europe.

The religious puritanism of the Hussites brought a reaction against artistic literature, and their chief contribution to it was the purification of the Czech language of Germanisms and archaisms, and the production of a number of interesting polemical works. The Hussite Wars served to cut Bohemia off from Humanism and other intellectual trends of the Renaissance, which entered belatedly in the latter part of the fifteenth and in the sixteenth centuries. It was once fashionable to proclaim the sixteenth century as the great age of Czech literature, but recent investigators have shown that the Czech Humanists relied too much on classical models for their syntax, style, rhetorical devices, and subject matter, and were often neglectful of the artistic and ideological needs of their people. Only the Humanists of the Protestant sect of Czech Brethren were partly free from these weaknesses, and, in the writings of Jan Blahoslav amd, above all, Jan Amos Komenský (Comenius), succeeded in advancing the national literary tradition. The Czech Brethren also created the great *Kralická Bible* (1579-1593), a work which embodied the highest stylistic level of its time and, but for the loss of national independence which came early in the seventeenth century, might have played a role in Czech literature comparable to that of the King James Bible or the Bible of Luther. But the period of subjugation to Austria brought a rapid decline, and Czech as a written language came close to extinction. Literature survived, but in the narrow frame of oral tradition, or in the forms of the Baroque religious poetry cultivated under the Counter-Reformation. A process of Germanization of the cities set in, and the Czech scholar Dobrovský, the father of comparative Slavic studies, feared at the beginning of the nineteenth century that he was studying a language which might soon cease to exist.

But forces were working in the opposite direction. Though the cities were largely Germanized, the country remained Czech, and from it there came a series of young patriots, who, influenced by the ideas of the French Revolution and the ethnic philosophy of Herder, sought to revive Czech literature and Czech national culture. Their efforts were at first hesitating and largely imitative. It was necessary to re-create the Czech literary language, provide forms for literary creation, and stimulate national consciousness with slogans and propaganda works. To these ends they translated models from foreign literatures, studied Old Czech literature, created a Czech dictionary, and even forged "great epic poems of antiquity," in order to prove that Czech had a great literary tradition and the Czechs a great past. They succeeded in establishing a national press, and by the 1830's, with Mácha and Erben, in producing a Romantic literature on a level comparable with the rest of Europe. By 1848 their numbers had grown so great that they could threaten the Hapsburg power itself. Harsh reaction followed their defeat, but with the 1860's there began a new movement, far deeper and broader in its effects, to convert the whole of the Czech nation, not only its intellectuals, to the patriotic cause. With this end in view, a national theatre was created, Czech schools founded, and a Czech encyclopedia compiled. Nationalist influence in literature was strong, and for a time Czech literature suffered from a certain provincialism (though a chief source was the unloved foreign model, German literature!); to Nationalism during the 1880's there was opposed literary cosmopolitanism and Parnassianism, bringing in new trends from abroad and providing the premises for the development of modern Czech literature. Realism as a conscious movement came belatedly to Bohemia during the 1880's, and, under the leadership of Masaryk, provided a greater immediate stimulus in the fields of philosophy, science, politics and criticism than in literature itself. Stronger in its effects on literature was Symbolism, which produced a number of original Czech poets, among them Otokar Březina.

Prose had lagged far behind poetry in Czech literary development, and not until the 1920's did Czech literature create a prose which could command international attention, notably in the works of Karel Čapek, who applied the American philosophy of pragmatism to literature. Other writers, though less known abroad, were no less great: Vladislav Vančura, a master of ornate prose style, full of archaisms and unusual turns of speech, and Ivan Olbracht, who studied the primitive life of Ruthenians and Jews in Trans-Carpathian Russia and infused their lore and superstition with new psychological reality and dramatic intensity. There were also experimentalists, especially in poetry, and surrealism and poetism were leading movements of the late 1920's.

Unfortunately, this era now seems to have come to a decisive end. Though Czech poetry has remained on a high technical level, Czech prose has lost its best writers. Čapek, Hašek and Vančura are now dead, while Olbracht and Jaroslav Durych have practically ceased to write. The generation of younger writers which might have succeeded them is now divided: some are in voluntary exile, others are silent, others are struggling to adjust their creation to the needs of the new regime. That

3

such adjustment requires a complete change of literary orientation, the new leaders themselves have not been slow to proclaim. It remains to be seen whether the writers of today can
satisfactorily adapt themselves to such a demand.

It is characteristic of the strongly ideological, at times
even didactic cast of Czech literature, that the three Czech
writers who have been most influential and are best known outside Bohemia are all men more renowned for their philosophic
or religious thought than for their purely literary accomplishments. Of the latter the world knows little or nothing. Jan Hus
reformed Czech prose style, purifying the language of Germanisms and archaisms, created the modern Czech alphabet, and
wrote in the colloquial language of the people. Jan Amos
Komenský, most noted as a philosopher of education, wrote inspired laments on the fate of his unhappy land, subject to the
Hapsburgs. Tomáš Garrigue Masaryk, though not himself a writer
of belles-lettres, helped perhaps more than any other man to
lay the foundation for modern Czech literature. He brought new
scientific trends and a spirit of realistic scepticism to his
fellow-countrymen, and himself led the attack on the forged
manuscripts which had supposedly constituted the "great Czech
literature of antiquity," thus ridding the past of a false,
romantic coloring, and leading to a re-evaluation of the true
nature of the Czech ideological and literary tradition.

It is significant that these three men all solved one of
the most difficult problems of Czech thought, indeed of the
thought of any small nation: they succeeded in combining nationalistic patriotism with an enlightened spirit of internationalism. Hus found this synthesis in a re-emphasis of spiritual
values and in the unity of the true Church, made manifest to
all men through teaching in the vernacular tongue. Komenský
found it in a union of patriotic activity and international
philosophic endeavour. Masaryk discovered it in the need to
re-orientate the provincial Czech world of the 1880's to internationalism and the modern critical spirit, so that Bohemia
might grow to a stature deserving of independence. It is in
this attempt to synthesize national culture and tradition with
the international and cosmopolitan that one may see the eternal
dynamic problem of Czech literary art and philosophic thought.

The American student who seeks a comprehensive knowledge of
Czech literature as a whole may well be disappointed with the
existing histories of that literature. With but rare exceptions, they are compilations, in which there is often too
little attempt to interpret, assay, or to link isolated literary phenomena. These defects are in part characteristic even
of Josef and Arne Novák's *Přehledné dějiny literatury české*
and its later abridgement, *Stručné dějiny literatury české*, at

present the standard history of Czech literature, a work intended more for reference than for continuous reading. Of the
older histories, Jaroslav Vlček's *Dějiny české literatury* is
now antiquated, as is partly the case with Jan Jakubec' *Dějiny
literatury české*, which ends with the middle of the nineteenth
century, though it contains much valuable material on the
early literature. Arne Novák's *Dějiny české literatury* (revised as *Dějiny českého písemnictví*; also available in German)
does, in the introduction, attempt to cope with the problem of
a characterization of the literature as a whole, but the analysis, otherwise brilliant, is weakened by its appeal to the
vague concept of a "Czech national character," and there is no
attempt to relate this "national character" to fundamental
causes which might have produced it. As a connected survey of
the whole of Czech literature, Hanuš Jelínek's *Histoire de la
littérature tchèque* is doubtless the most interesting reading,
but, in spite of its three volumes, it is hardly complete.
František Chudoba's *A Short Survey of Czech Literature* is all
too brief, while Franz Lützow's *A History of Bohemian Literature* is out of date and sadly incomplete even in its treatment
of the nineteenth century.

Nor are many histories and individual studies satisfactory
from the purely literary point of view. Nineteenth century investigators were often concered primarily with questions of
philology, national ideology or cultural history, and only
secondarily with the analysis and evaluation of works of literature as such. The reader will miss the latter type of analysis in the studies of Vlček, Hanuš, Jakubec and many others of
the older school. He may well be surprised at the all too widespread tendency of Czech critics to evaluate a work of literature as great purely because it expresses a positive nationalistic ideology, a tendency characteristic of the otherwise excellent work of Albert Pražák. He will be equally disappointed
if he looks for attempts to explain literature on the basis of
strict historical, political or economic causation. Nor will
he find, outside of the Parnassians, exponents of the doctrine
of "art for art's sake."

A revolution in modern Czech criticism was led by František
Xaver Šalda, the most gifted of Czech critics. Šalda created
the terminology of Czech literary criticism. He sought to free
Czech literature from the bonds of the attitude of "l'art pour
l'art" of the Parnassian poet Vrchlický and his school, as
well as from the widespread view that art and literature need
serve only for the creation and propagation of an active nationalistic ideology. He taught that literature and art were
completely serious activities, not divorced from life, but at
its very heart and center, a spiritual value on a level with

5

religion itself, one by no means shut off from the moral and
social demands of life, but in continual contact with them.
He attempted the difficult task of synthesizing the moral and
social responsibilities of art with its purely formal and sen-
sual appeal, thus uniting the older, sharply hostile views of
the Parnassians and the Nationalists. Unfortunately, much of
Šalda's attention was devoted to world literature, and he
never succeeded in creating a synthetic picture of Czech literature as a whole. His approach was likewise deficient from
the historical point of view. Similarly, Otokar Fischer, almost alone among modern Czech critics to apply the methods of
psychoanalysis and modern psychology to literary science, was
too occupied with the study and translation of German literature to contribute more than a handful of brilliant studies
and essays to Czech criticism.

A most important contribution to modern Czech literary
science was made by the so-called Structuralists, a group of
estheticians and scholars strongly influenced by Russian For-
malism, and gathered about the Prague Linguistic Circle and
the review, *Slovo a slovesnost.* Led by Roman Jakobson, Jan
Mukařovský and Mikuláš Bakoš in Slovakia, these men placed a
new emphasis on the objective analysis of literary form, considered as an entity existing and developing independently of
the psychology of the creator. They brought new, more refined
methods to the study of formal problems, such as prosody, literary style and the use of language, and indicated new direc-
tions for the re-evaluation of Czech literary history. Unfortunately, the activity of this school was cut short by the war,
and none of its members succeeded in creating a work which
dealt with more than certain specialized questions of literary
history and criticism.

The present scene shows confusion in the attempt to adopt
a Marxist-Leninist-Stalinist approach to literature piecemeal,
and the difficulty of applying "Russian" standards to Czech
literature, in essence quite different from Russian. A new emphasis on "nationalistic" literature and on the evaluation of
literature in regard to its patriotic or pan-Slavic motivation
is also evident.

BIBLIOGRAPHY
CZECH LITERATURE AND RELATED FIELDS

An asterisk (*) indicates works which also pertain to Slovak literature and related fields.

See also works marked with a double asterisk (**) in the Slovak section of the bibliography.

GENERAL WORKS
Historical and Cultural Background

1. Denis, Ernest, *La Bohême depuis la Montagne-Blanche*, I-II, Paris, 1903 and 1930.

*2. Kerner, R.J., ed., *Czechoslovakia*, Berkeley, Cal., 1945.

*3. Krofta, Kamil, *A Short History of Czechoslovakia*, London, 1926 and 1935; New York, 1934.

*4. Mathesius, Vilém, ed., *Co daly naše země Evropě a lidstvu*, I-II, Prague, 1939-40.

*5. Novotný, Václav and Otakar Odložilík, eds., *Dějiny, Československá vlastivěda*, Vol. IV, Prague, 1932.

6. Novotný, Václav, J.V.Šimák, Josef Šusta, F.M.Bartoš and Rudolf Urbánek, *České dějiny*, Vol. I, Parts 1-5; Vol. II, Parts 1-6; Vol. III, Parts 1-3, Prague, Jan Leichter, 1912-48 (covers Czech history from its beginnings to 1462).

*7. Odložilík, Otakar, *Nástin československých dějin*, London, 1942; Prague, 1946.

*8. Pekař, Josef, *Dějiny československé pro nejvyšší třídy škol*, Prague, 1921 and 1937.

*9. Polišenský, J.V., *History of Czechoslovakia in Outline*, Prague, 1948.

10. Schwarz, Henry F., "Bohemia under the Hapsburgs,"

7

A *Handbook of Slavic Studies*, ed. L.I.Strakhovsky, Cambridge, Mass., 1949, pp. 243-270.

*11. Seton-Watson, R.W., *A History of the Czechs and the Slovaks*, London, 1943.

*12. Thomson, S. Harrison, *Czechoslovakia in European History*, Princeton, 1944.

*13. Král, Josef, *Československá filosofie*, Prague, 1937.

14. Pražák, Albert, *Národ se bránil. Obrany národa a jazyka českého*, Prague, 1946.

Historical Surveys of Czech Literature

15. Chudoba, František, *A Short Survey of Czech Literature*, London, 1924.

16. Jakubec, Jan, *Dějiny literatury české*, Prague, 1911; enlarged edition, I, 1929; II, 1934.

17. Jakubec, Jan and Arne Novák, *Geschichte der Čechischen Literatur*, Leipzig, 1907 and 1913.

18. Jelínek, Hanuš, *Histoire de la littérature tchèque*, I-III, Paris, 1930-35.

19. Lützow, Franz, *A History of Bohemian Literature*, London, 1899 and 1907.

20. Novák, Arne, "Dějiny české literatury," *Československá vlastivěda*, Prague, 1933, VII, 7-208. Revised as *Dějiny českého písemnictví*, ed. A. Grund, Prague, 1946. German edition as "Die Tschechische Literatur," *Handbuch der Literaturwissenschaft*, ed. O. Walzel, Potsdam, 1931, XVIII, 1-114.

*21. Novák, Josef and Arne Novák, *Přehledné dějiny literatury české*, Olomouc, 1936-39. Abridged edition: *Stručné dějiny literatury české*, ed. R. Havel and A. Grund, Olomouc, 1946.

*22. Vlček, Jaroslav, *Dějiny české literatury*, I-IV, Prague, 1892-1914; 1931; 1940.

*23. Sezima, Karel and Antonín Veselý, eds., *Výbor z krásné prózy československé*, I-VIII, Prague, 1932.

8

Specialized Questions

24. Máchal, Jan, *Dějiny českého dramata*, Prague, 1917 and 1929.

25. Havránek, Bohuslav, "Vývoj spisovného jazyka českého," *Československá vlastivěda*, Prague, 1936, Second Series, I, 1-144.

26. Jakobson, Roman, *Základy českého verše*, Prague, 1926.

27. Král, Josef, *O prosodii české*, ed. Jan Jakubec, Prague, 1924.

28. Mukařovský, Jan, *Kapitoly z české poetiky*, I-III, Prague, 1948-49 (Vol. I treats theory of Czech prosody and poetic style; Vol. II contains important studies on Hálek, Čapek, Vančura, etc.; Vol. III is devoted to Mácha).

29. Horák, Jiří, "Národopis československý," *Československá vlastivěda*, Prague, 1933, II, 305-473.

30. Václavek, Bedřich, *Písemnictví a lidová tradice*, Prague, 1947.

31. Wellek, René, "The Two Traditions of Czech Literature," *Slavic Studies*, ed. A. Kaun and E.J.Simmons, Ithaca, N.Y., 1943, pp. 213-228.

THE MIDDLE AGES
(NINTH TO FOURTEENTH CENTURIES)

32. Krofta, Kamil, "Bohemia to the Extinction of the Přemyslides," *Cambridge Medieval History*, New York, 1929, VI, 422-447.

33. Thomson, S.Harrison, "Medieval Bohemia," *A Handbook of Slavic Studies*, ed. L.I.Strakhovsky, Cambridge, Mass., 1949, pp. 97-121.

34. Tadra, Ferdinand, *Kulturní styky Čech s cizinou až do válek husitských*, Prague, 1897.

35. Jakobson, Roman, *Moudrost starých Čechů*, New York, 1943.

36. Vilikovský, Jan, *Písemnictví českého středověku*, Prague, 1948.

*37. Pastrnek, František, *Dějiny slovanských apoštolů Cyrilla a Methodia*, Prague, 1902.

38. Jakobson, Roman, "Verš staročeský," *Československá vlasti-věda*, Prague, 1934, III, 429-459.

39. Flajšhans, Václav, ed., *Nejstarši památky jazyka a písemnictví českého*, Vol. I, *Prolegomena a texty*, Prague, 1903.

40. Chaloupecký, Václav, ed., *Na úsvitu křesťanství. Z naší literární tvorby doby románské v stol. IX-XIII.*, Prague, 1942. (Anthology).

41. Jakobson, Roman, *Nejstarší české písně duchovní*, Prague, 1929.

42. Nejedlý, Zdeněk, *Dějiny předhusitského zpěvu v Čechách*, Prague, 1904.

43. Pražák, Albert, *Staročeská báseň o Alexandru Velikém*, Prague, 1945.

44. Máchal, Jan, ed., *Staročeské skladby dramatické původu liturgického (text i rozbor)*, Prague, 1908.

45. Černý, Václav, *Staročeská milostná lyrika*, Prague, 1948.

46. Vilikovský, Jan, ed., *Próza z doby Karla Čtvrtého*, Prague, 1938. (Anthology).

47. -----, ed., *Staročeská lyrika*, Prague, 1940. (Anthology).

48. Hrabák, Josef, ed., *Staročeské satiry*, Prague, 1947. (Anthology).

49. -----, ed., *Smilova škola, Studie Pražského linguistického kroužku, III*, Prague, 1941.

50. Gebauer, Jan, *O životě a spisích Tomáše ze Štítného*, Prague, 1923.

THE HUSSITE MOVEMENT AND THE CZECH REFORMATION
(FIFTEENTH AND SIXTEENTH CENTURIES)

51. Denis, Ernest, *Huss et la guerre des Hussites,* Paris, 1878.

52. Krofta, Kamil, "Bohemia in the Fifteenth Century,"
    Cambridge Medieval History, New York, 1936, VIII,
    65-115.

53. Bartoš, František M., *Husitství a cizina,* Prague, 1931.

54. Losserth, Johann, *Huss und Wiclif; zur Genesis der hussi-
    tischen Lehre,* rev. ed., Munich and Berlin, 1925.

55. Odložilík, Otakar, "Wycliffe's Influence upon Central and
    Eastern Europe," *Slavonic and East European Review,*
    VII, 21 (March, 1929), pp. 634-648.

56. Flajšhans, Václav, *M. J. Hus,* Prague, 1915.

57. Lützow, Franz, *The Life and Times of Master Jan Hus,* New
    York, 1909.

58. Masaryk, Tomáš G., *Jan Hus. Naše obrození a naše refor-
    mace,* Prague, 1896.

59. Novotný, Václav and Vlastimil Kybal, *Mistr Jan Hus,* I-IV,
    Prague, 1919-27.

60. Spinka, Matthew, *John Hus and the Czech Reform,* Chicago,
    1941.

61. Lützow, Franz, *The Hussite Wars,* New York, 1914.

62. Jakobson, Roman, "Úvahy o básnictví doby husitské," *Slovo
    a slovesnost,* Vol. II (1936), pp. 1-21.

63. Nejedlý, Zdeněk, *Dějiny husitského zpěvu za válek husit-
    ských,* Prague, 1907.

64. Odložilík, Otakar, "George of Poděbrady and Bohemia to
    the Pacification of Silesia," *University of Colorado
    Studies,* I, 3 (1941), pp. 265-288.

65. -----, "Problems of the Reign of George of Poděbrady,"
    Slavonic and East European Review, Vol. XX (1941),
    pp. 206-222.

66. Müller, Joseph T., *Geschichte der Böhmischen Brüder*, I-III, Herrnhut, 1922-1931.

67. Goll, Jaroslav, *Chelčický a Jednota v patnáctém století*, Prague, 1916.

68. Truhlář, Josef, *Počátky humanismu v Čechách*, Prague, 1892.

69. Truhlář, Antonín, *Rukovět k písemnictví humanistickému, zvláště básnickému, v Čechách a na Moravě ve stol. XVI.*, ed. K. Hrdina, Vol. I, Prague, 1918.

70. Krofta, Kamil, *O bratrském dějepisectví*, Prague, 1946.

71. Novotný, Václav, ed., *Sborník Blahoslavův*, Přerov, 1923.

72. Václavek, Bedřich, ed., *Historie utěšené a kratochvilné. Výbor z české krásné prózy XVI. a XVII. století*, Prague, 1941.

BAROQUE LITERATURE
(SEVENTEENTH AND EIGHTEENTH CENTURIES)

73. Denis, Ernest, *La fin de l'indépendence bohême*, I-II, Paris, 1890 and 1930.

74. Heyberger, Anna, *Jean Amos Comenius (Komenský); sa vie et et son oeuvre d'éducateur, Travaux de l'Institut d'études slaves*, Vol. III, Paris, 1928.

75. Kvacsala, Johann (Kvačala, Ján), *Johann Amos Comenius. Seine Leben und seine Schriften*, Leipzig, 1892.

76. Novák, Jan V., *Jan Amos Komenský; jeho život a spisy*, Prague, 1920; second edition with supplement by Josef Hendrich, Prague, 1932.

77. Spinka, Matthew, *John Amos Comenius, That Incomparable Moravian*, Chicago, 1943.

78. Bitnar, Vilém, *O českém baroku slovesném*, Prague, 1932.

79. -----, *Postavy a problémy českého baroku literárního*, Prague, 1939.

80. Šalda, František X., "O literárním baroku cizím i domácím," *Studie literárně historické a kritické*, Prague, 1937.

81. Vašica, Josef, *České literární baroko*, Prague, 1938.

82. Bitnar, Vilém, ed., *Zrození barokového básníka. Anthologie z přírodní lyriky*, Prague, 1940.

*83. Kalista, Zdeněk, ed., *České baroko; studie, texty, poznámky*, Prague, 1940.

84. -----, ed., *Z legend českého baroku*, Olomouc, 1934. (Anthology).

85. Bobek, Wladyslaw, *Bohuslav Balbín*, Bratislava, 1933.

THE CZECH REVIVAL AND THE NINETEENTH CENTURY
General Works

86. Leger, Louis, *La Renaissance tchèque au dix-neuvième siècle*, Paris, 1911.

87. Masaryk, Tomáš G., *Česká otázka. Snahy a tužby národního obrození*, Prague, 1895 and 1908.

88. Pražák, Albert, *České obrození*, Prague, 1948.

89. -----, *O národ*, Prague, 1946.

90. Szykowski, Marjan, *Polská účast v českém národním obrození*, I-III, Prague, 1931-46.

*91. Smith, Horatio, ed., *Columbia Dictionary of Modern European Literature*, New York, 1947 (contains articles on modern Czech and Slovak literature by René Wellek; also many articles by Wellek on individual writers).

*92. Vlček, Jaroslav, ed., *Literatura česká devatenáctého století*, I-III, Prague, 1902-07; Volumes I and II revised, ed. Jan Jakubec, Prague, 1911, 1917. Of especial importance are articles on Dobrovský, Jungmann, Hanka, Čelakovský, J.J.Langer, Havlíček, Němcová, Neruda and Hálek.

*93. Čapek, Jan B., *Československá literatura toleranční, 1781-1861*, I-II, Prague, 1933.

94. Harkins, William E., *The Russian Folk Epos in Czech Literature, 1800-1900*, New York, 1950.

95. Murko, Matthias, *Deutsche Einflüsse auf die Anfänge der Böhmischen Romantik*, Graz, 1897.

96. Fischer, Otokar, *Duše a dílo*, Prague, 1929.

97. ----, *Slovo a svět*, Prague, 1937.

98. Novák, Arne, *Duch a národ*, Prague, 1936.

99. ----, *Krajané a sousedé. Kniha studií a podobizen*, Prague, 1922 and 1930.

100. ----, *Zvony domova. Kniha studií a podobizen*. Prague, 1916.

101. Šalda, František X., *Časové a nadčasové*, Prague, 1936

102. ----, *Duše a dílo*. Podobizny a medaliony, Prague, 1913; rev. ed., 1915 and 1922.

103. ----, *Studie literárně historické a kritické*, Prague, 1937.

104. Vrchlický, Jaroslav, *Studie a podobizny*, Prague, 1897.

105. ----, *Nové studie a podobizny*, Prague, 1897.

106. Fischer, Otakar, "Činohra Národního divadla do roku 1900," *Dějiny Národního divadla*, Vol. IV, Prague, 1933.

107. Träger, Josef, "Počátky českého divadla," *Československá vlastivěda*, Prague, 1935, VII, 323-356.

108. Tille, Václav, *České pohádky do roku 1848*, Prague, 1909.

109. Mukařovský, Jan, "Obecné zásady a vývoj novočeského verše," *Československá vlastivěda*, Prague, 1943, III, 376-429. (Reprinted in Vol. I of *Kapitoly z české poetiky*, Prague, 1948).

110. Procházka, František S., ed., *Česká epika*, Prague, 1924. (Anthology).

111. ----, ed., *Česká lyrika*, Prague, 1926. (Anthology).

The Age of the Enlightenment
and the Czech Revival

112. Bílý, František, *Od kolébky našeho obrození*, Prague, 1904.

113. Hanuš, Josef, *Národní museum a naše obrození*, I-II, Prague, 1921-23.

114. Horák, Jiří, M. Murko and M. Weingart, eds., *Josef Dobrovský, 1753-1829*, Prague, 1929.

115. Ludvíkovský, Jaroslav, *Dobrovského klasická humanita*, Bratislava, 1933.

116. Novák, Arne, *Josef Dobrovský*, Prague, 1928.

117. Weingart, Miloš, "Joseph Dobrovský, the Patriarch of Slavonic Studies," *Slavonic and East European Review*, VIII, 21 (March, 1929), pp. 663-675.

118. Vlček, Jaroslav, *První novočeská škola básnická*, Prague, 1896.

119. Vodička, Felix, *Počátky krásné prózy novočeské*, Prague, 1948.

120. Chalupný, Emanuel, *Josef Jungmann*, Prague, 1909.

121. Zelený, Václav, *Život Josefa Jungmanna*, Prague, 1873 and 1881.

122. Bartoš, František M., *Rukopisy*, Prague, 1936.

123. Gebauer, Jan, *Poučení o padělaných rukopisích královédvorském a zelenohorském*, Prague, 1888.

124. Jakobson, Roman, "Pamjati Vjačeslava Vjačeslavoviča Ganki," *Central'naja Evropa*, Vol. IV (1931), pp. 268-275.

*125. Jakubec, Jan, *O životě a působení Jana Kollára*, Prague, 1893.

126. Máchal, Jan, *Snahy F.L.Čelakovského o obnovu české literatury*, Prague, 1899.

127. Jirát, Vojtěch, ed., *Lyrika českého obrození*, Prague, 1940. (Anthology).

128. Novák, Arne, ed., *Literatura českého klasicismu obrozen-*
     ského, Prague, 1933. (Anthology).

129. Očadlík, Mirko, ed., *Zpěv českého obrození (1750–1866)*,
     Prague, 1940. (Anthology).

Czech Romanticism

130. Fischer, Josef L., *Myšlenka a dílo Františka Palackého*,
     I-II, Prague, 1926-27.

131. Masaryk, Tomáš G., *Palackého idea národa českého*, Prague,
     1912.

132. Pekař, Josef, *František Palacký*, Prague, 1912.

133. Vlček, Jaroslav, *Pavel Josef Šafařík*, Prague, 1895.

134. Mukařovský, Jan, *Máchův Máj. Estetická studie*. Prague,
     1928. (Reprinted in Vol. III of *Kapitoly z české*
     poetiky, Prague, 1949).

135. ————, ed., *Torso a tajemství Máchova díla*, Prague, 1936.

136. Novák, Arne, ed., *Karel Hynek Mácha, osobnost, dílo, ohlas.*
     Sborník k 100. výročí Máchovy smrti, Prague, 1937.

137. Pražák, Albert, *K.H.Mácha*, Kolín, 1936.

138. Šalda, František X., *Mácha snivec a buřič*, Prague, 1936.

139. Vyskočil, Albert, *Básník. Studie máchovské otázky*, Prague,
     1936.

140. Wellek, René, "Mácha and Byron," *Slavonic and East Euro-*
     pean Review, XV, 44 (Jan., 1937), pp. 400-412.

141. Grund, Antonín, *Karel Jaromír Erben*, Prague, 1935.

142. Jakobson, Roman, "Poznámky k dílu Erbenovu," *Slovo a slo-*
     vesnost, Vol. I (1935), pp. 152-164, 218-229.

143. Hýsek, Miloslav, *Josef Kajetán Tyl*, Prague, 1926.

144. Hanuš, Josef, *Život a spisy Václava Bolemíra Nebeského*,
     Prague, 1896.

145. Masaryk, Tomáš G., *Karel Havlíček. Snahy a tužby politi-*

ckého probuzení, Prague, 1896 and 1904.

146. Chalupný, Emanuel, *Havlíček; prostředí, osobnost a dílo*, Prague, 1929.

*147. Šalda, František X., *Básnický typ Boženy Němcové*, Turnova, 1935.

*148. Tille, Václav, *Božena Němcová*, Prague, 1911; fifth edition, revised by M.Novotný, Prague, 1939.

*149. Pražák, Albert, "Czechs and Slovaks in the Revolution of 1848," *Slavonic and East European Review*, Vol. V, 15 (March, 1926), pp. 565-579.

*150. -----, "Czechs and Slovaks after the Revolution of 1848," *Slavonic and East European Review*, VI, 16 (Jan., 1927), pp. 119-129.

151. Novák, Arne, *Jan Neruda*, Prague, 1910 and 1920.

Cosmopolitanism and Nationalism

152. Bačkovský, František, *Přehled písemnictví českého doby nejnovější*, Prague, 1899.

153. Vlček, Jaroslav, *Několik kapitolek z dějin naší slovesnosti*, Prague, 1912.

154. -----, *Nové kapitoly z dějin literatury české*, Prague, 1912.

155. -----, *Několik kapitolek z dějin naší poesie*, Prague, 1898.

156. Hýsek, Miloslav, *Literární Morava v letech 1849 až 1885*, Prague, 1911.

157. Flajšhans, Václav, *Svatopluk Čech, dílo a člověk*, Prague, 1906.

158. Jednota Svatopluka Čecha, *Svatopluku Čechovi (sborník)*, Prague, 1946.

159. Novák, Arne, *Svatopluk Čech, dílo a osobnost*, I-II, Prague, 1921-23.

160. Jensen, Alfred, *Jaroslav Vrchlický, en litterär studie*,

Stockholm, 1904; Czech translation by Arnošt Kraus, Prague, 1908.

161. Krejčí, František V., *Jaroslav Vrchlický*, Prague, 1913.

162. Tichý, Vítězslav, *Jaroslav Vrchlický; život*, Prague, 1947.

163. Chalupný, Emanuel, *J. V. Sládek a lumírovská doba české literatury*, Prague, 1916.

164. Strejček, Ferdinand, *Josef Václav Sládek, jak žil, pracoval a trpěl*, Prague, 1916.

165. Kvapil, Josef Š., *Gotický Zeyer*, Prague, 1942.

166. Voborník, Jan, *Julius Zeyer*, Prague, 1907.

167. Krejčí, Karel, *Jakub Arbes*, Moravská Ostrava and Prague, 1946.

168. Šalda, František X., *Moderní literatura česká*, Prague, 1909 and 1920.

169. Máchal, Jan, *Boje o nové směry v české literatuře, 1880-1900*, Prague, 1926.

170. —————, *O českém románu novodobém*, Prague, 1902; rev. ed., Prague, 1930.

171. Masaryk, Tomáš G., *Naše nynější krise. Pod strany staročeské a počátkové směrů nových*, Prague, 1895.

172. Herben, Jan, *T. G. Masaryk. Sa vie. Sa politique. Sa philophie*, Prague, 1923.

173. —————, *T. G. Masaryk*, I-III, Prague, 1926-27.

174. Hromádka, Josef L., *Masaryk*, Prague, 1930.

175. Nejedlý, Zdeněk, *T. G. Masaryk*, I-IV, Prague, 1931-37.

176. Selver, Paul. *Masaryk, a Biography*, London, 1940.

*177. Hanč, Josef, "Czechoslovakia," *A Handbook of Slavic Studies*, ed. L.I.Strakhovsky, Cambridge, Mass., 1949, pp. 572-603.

*178. Polák, Karel, *Československá literatura, 1890-1935*, Prague, 1936.

179. Václavek, Bedřich, *Česká literatura II. století*, Prague, 1947.

180. Götz, František, *Jasnící se horizont*, Prague, 1926.

181. Píša, Antonín M., *Směry a cíle*, Prague, 1927.

182. Václavek, Bedřich, *Od umění k tvorbě*, Prague, 1928.

183. Vyskočil, Albert, *Básníkova cesta*, Prague, 1927.

184. ------, *Básníkovo slovo. Kritické studie*. Prague, 1933.

185. Tille, Václav, "Činohra Národního divadla od roku 1900 do převratu," *Dějiny Národního divadla*, Vol. V, Prague, 1935.

Realism and Symbolism in Modern Poetry

186. Martínek, Vojtěch, *J.S.Machar. Přehled jeho básnického díla*, Prague, 1912.

187. Hýsek, Miloslav, *Tři kapitoly o Petru Bezručovi*, Brno, 1934.

188. Martínek, Vojtěch, *Petr Bezruč. Literární studie*, Moravská Ostrava, 1924.

189. Králík, Oldřich, *Otokar Březina, 1892-1907. Logika jeho díla*, Prague, 1948.

190. Selver, Paul, *Otokar Březina, a Study in Czech Literature*, Oxford, 1921.

191. Staněk, Josef and Jaroslav Durych, *Otokar Březina. Studie literárně historické*, Přerov, 1918 and 1931.

192. Píša, Antonín M., *Otakar Theer*, I-II, Prague, 1928-33.

193. Kruh českých spisovatelů, *Nová česká poesie*, Prague, 1907. (Anthology).

194. Hora, Josef, *Karel Toman*, Prague, 1935.

195. Novák, Arne, *Viktor Dyk*, Prague, 1936.

196. Rutte, Miroslav, *Viktor Dyk. Portrét básníka*, Prague, 1931.

197. Václavek, Bedřich, *Stanislav K. Neumann, 1875-1935*, Prague, 1935.

Czech Literature after the First World War

198. Bittner, Konrad, *Das Tschechische Schriftum der Nachkriegszeit*, Munich, 1939.

199. Kunc, Jaroslav, ed., *Slovník soudobých českých spisovatelů. Krásné písemnictví v letech 1918-1945*, I-II, Prague, 1946.

200. Durych, Jaroslav, *Ejhle, člověk!* Prague, 1926.

201. Hostovský, Egon, "The Czech Novel between the Two World Wars," *Slavonic and East European Review*, Vol. XXI (Nov., 1943), pp. 78-96.

202. Novák, Arne, "Czech Literature in and after the War," *Slavonic and East European Review*, II, 4 (June, 1923), pp. 114-132.

203. Šalda, František X., *Krásná literatura česká v prvním desetiletí republiky*, Prague, 1930.

204. ------, *Mladé zápasy*, Prague, 1934.

205. Wellek, René, "Twenty Years of Czech Literature, 1918-1938," *Slavonic and East European Review*, XVII, 50 (Jan., 1939), pp. 329-342.

206. Černý, Václav, *Karel Čapek*, Prague, 1936.

207. Elton, Oliver, "Karel Čapek: Short Tales and Fantasies; Later Novels," *Essays and Addresses*, New York and London, 1939, pp. 151-190.

208. Manning, Clarence A., "Karel Capek," *South Atlantic Quarterly*, XL, 3 (July, 1941), pp. 236-242.

209. van Santen, Aimé, *Over Karel Čapek*, Amsterdam, 1949.

210. Wellek, René, "Karel Čapek," *Slavonic and East European Review*, XV, 43 (July, 1936), pp. 191-206.

211. Píša, Antonín M., *Ivan Olbracht*, Prague, 1949.

212. Götz, František, *Anarchie v nejmladší české poesie*, Brno, 1922.

213. -----, *Básnický dnešek. Vývoj perspektivy nové české poesie*, Prague, 1931.

214. Nezval, Vítězslav, *Moderní básnické směry*, Prague, 1937.

215. Šalda, František X., *Kritické glosy k nové české poesii*, Prague, 1939.

216. -----, *O nejmladši poesii české*, Prague, 1928.

217. Götz, František, *František Xaver Šalda*, Prague, 1937.

SELECTED LIST OF CZECH PERIODICALS
DEVOTED TO
LITERARY SCHOLARSHIP AND CRITICISM

Athenaum; listy pro literaturu a kritiku vědeckou, Prague, Vols. I-X (1883-93).

Bratislava, Učená společnost Šafaříkova, Prague and Bratislava, Vols. I-XI (1927-37).

Časopis Národního musea, Národní museum, Prague, Vol. I- (1827-). Also known as: *Časopis Českého museum*, *Časopis Museum království Českého*, and *Časopis Společnosti vlasteneckého museum v Čechách*.

Časopis pro moderní filologii a literaturu, Klub moderních filologů, Prague, I - (1911-).

Host, Brno, Vols. I-VIII (1921-29).

Kritický měsíčník, Prague, Vols. I-IX, X- (1935-42; 1945-)

Kritika, Prague, Vols. I-IV (1924-28).

Květy, Prague, Vols. I-LXXIII (1878-1916).

Listy filologické, Jednota českých filologů v Praze, Vol. I-
(1874-   ). From 1874 to 1886 called *Listy filologické
a paedogogické*.

Listy pro umění a kritiku, Prague, Vols I-IV (1933-37).

Literární noviny, Evropský literární klub, Prague, Vol. I-
(1928-   ).

Literární rozhledy, Prague, Vols. I-XV (1916-31).

Literatura; bibliograficko-vzdělavácí věstník, Prague, Vols.
I-XVI (1923-38).

Lumír, Literární odbor, Umělecké besedy, Prague, Vols. I-LXVII
(1873-1940).

Moderní revue, Prague, Vols. I-XXXI (1894-1925).

Naše doba, Prague, Vols. I-LVI (1893-1949).

Naše kniha; bibliografický věstník, Prague, Vols. I-XXIV
(1920-43).

Naše řeč, Prague, Vol. I-   (1917-   ).

Novina, Prague, Vols. I-IV (1908-12).

Osvěta; listy pro rozhled v umění, vědě a politice, Prague,
Vols. I-XLIX (1871-1919).

Rozhledy národohospodářské, sociální, politické a literární,
Prague, Vols. I-XVII (1892-1909).

Řád, Prague, Vols. I-X (1935-44).

Slavia; časopis pro slovanskou filologii, Prague, Vols. I-
(1922-   ).

*Slavische Rundschau; berichtende und kritische Zeitschrift für
das geistige Leben der slavischen Völker*, Slavisches
Institut in Prag, Vols. I-XII (1929-40).

Slovanský přehled, Prague, Vol. I-   (1898-   ).

Slovesná věda; sborník pro literární historii, theorii literatury a literární kritiku, Prague, Vol. I- (1947-).

Slovo a slovesnost, Pražský linguistický kroužek, Prague, Vol. I- (1935-).

Šaldův zápisník, Prague, Vols. I–IX (1928–37).

Tvar, Prague, Vols. I–IV (1928–32).

Umělecký měsíčník, Prague, Vols. I–III (1911–14).

SLOVAK   LITERATURE

AND

RELATED   FIELDS

by

Klement Šimončič

PREFACE

It is important for the student of Slovak literary history to realize that, until quite recently, almost all major works on the history of Slovak literature, whether written in Slovak, Czech, or any other language, did not go fundamentally beyond the limits of biography and bibliography (hence a relative abundance of monographs!'. More often than not the authors of these works followed in their theory the standard concepts of "Kulturgeschichte," presenting at best the "history of ideas." Thus the most widely used histories of Slovak literature are little more than works on the general history of the Slovak people, its language, thought, politics and cultural development, illustrated with examples either from the literature in general or from artistic literature and folklore. Works of poetry and fiction are considered by such literary historians not as phenomena of the art of the language, but as "documents," as sources of information on the ethnic, religious, political, and even economic life of the country and its people. "History of literature" as thus conceived could only present a distorted picture of the significance and intrinsic value of any given fact of literature.

The foregoing is intended in no way to diminish the merits of such distinguished historians of Slovak literature as Jaroslav Vlček, Albert Pražák and others. Vlček's *Dejiny literatúry slovenskej*, first published in 1890, will forever remain a classic in its field. Enriched by the results of contemporary methodological research in the theory of literary history, Andrej Mráz's *Dejiny slovenskej literatúry* (1948) represents by far the most competent and up-to-date work on the history of Slovak literature.

• • • • •

Several fundamental theoretical problems, among them the definition of Slovak literature itself, face every historian of Slovak literature. What is Slovak literature? Is it everything which was ever written, propagated orally, or published in some form or another within the territory of Slovakia, regardless of the ethnic background or ideology of its author? Or is it everything written by Slovaks, whether they wrote in

Latin, Czech, or even in German or Magyar? It is obvious that for the older period of Slovak literary history, at least, with its relative paucity of purely esthetic works, all literary production, irrespective of function, must be taken into account. And so one historian of Slovak literature has stated that he considers the proper object of Slovak literary historiography to be: "any literary production by persons of Slovak origin, if such production was not in conflict with the spiritual needs and interests of the Slovak community." Others, however, have attempted to establish a periodization of Slovak literature based on the principle of immanent evolution of the artistic literature alone.

•••••

The beginnings of cultural life in the territory which was to become Slovakia coincided with Christianization and the arrival in the 1869's of the Apostles to the Slavs, Saints Constantine (Cyril) and Methodius, to the ninth-century European empire known as Great Moravia. The two brothers made (about 863) a Slavonic translation of liturgical texts and of the Gospel. During this Old Church Slavonic period, ideological stress was placed on the right of peoples to worship God in their own tongue. This emphasis on the use of the national tongue became a basic tenet of Slavic medieval literature, and was frequently evoked during the Reformation and Counter-Reformation and, at the end of the eighteenth century, even influenced the first organized attempts to standardize the Slovak literary language.

The period of Old Church Slavonic culture was of short duration in Slovakia. Divine services in Slavonic, first authorized by the Holy See about 880, were forbidden five years later. At the end of the ninth century the Great Moravian Empire was overrun by nomad Magyar tribes. After the tenth century both Slovakia and Hungary became part of the Western European social and cultural, if not political, world. Latin became the language of monasteries, of churches and schools, of feudal nobility and sovereigns.

The rule of Latin in Slovakia lasted, in fact, to the end of the eighteenth century. But in the mid-fifteenth century, with the arrival of Hussite armies from Bohemia, Czech became the official language, not only of the administration of many towns, but, for a time, of the Court of Hungary itself. More than two hundred documents from the fifteenth century alone are written either in classical Czech of the fourteenth century, or in a Czech strongly influenced by the Slovak spoken language of the period. During the seventeenth and eighteenth centuries more Czech writings were published on Slovak than on Czech soil.

For almost four centuries Czech remained the dominant literary language of the Protestant minority of the Slovak nation, though Latin continued to be the chief medium of communication in Catholic churches and schools, and, as in the West, was cultivated by scholars of both Catholic and Protestant faiths.

In literature the period of the Renaissance produced in Slovakia (1500-1650) mostly religious lyrics, historical epics, school dramas, sermons, catechetical works and works of didactic poetry, written for the most part in Latin.

The Reformation – as elsewhere – provided a great impetus for the creation of literature in the vernacular and for the creation of a Slovak standard language. Luther's reforms made the hymn an element of central importance in religious worship, and provided that it should be comprehensible for every worshipper, literate or not. Slovak Protestants found such hymns in the rich Hussite hymnal literature of the Czechs. In 1636 a great collection of Czech hymns was published in Slovakia by Jiří Třanovský, a Czech Protestant preacher, under the title of *Cithara Sanctorum*. This anthology was subsequently revised several times, and some 130 editions have appeared.

The needs of the Catholic Counter-Reformation called for an analogous hymnal for Catholics. In 1665 there was published at the University of Trnava, the center of the Slovak Counter-Reformation, a book which, save for its title, was written in Slovak. The editor of *Cantus Catholici* observed on the title page that the work contained "Pýsne Katholicke, Latinské y Slowenské, Nowé y Starodawné" (Catholic Hymns, Latin and Slovak, New and Ancient).

Both works were of paramount importance in view of subsequent historical developments in Slovakia. The Catholic publications of the seventeenth century were unable to compete with the beauty of classical Czech, which became the chief vehicle of Protestant proselytizing in Slovakia. *Cantus Catholici* contained a preface which recalled (inaccurately) that it was Rome which had first permitted, in the ninth century, the use of the Slavonic language in divine services. The Catholics thus strove to establish historical continuity in their attempts to make a more extended use of the vernacular in higher communicative and esthetic functions.

In literature the seventeenth and eighteenth centuries in Slovakia were characterized by a plethora of religious writings, both Protestant and Catholic, mostly of polemic and apologetic character. But, by the end of the seventeenth century, secular poetry appeared, written either in "biblical" (Hussite) Czech or in the Slovak vernacular. A striking feature of this literature is that a very large proportion of it, whether religious or secular in content, whether Latin, Czech or Slovak in language, was in verse. It is also important to note that the literary theories of the Baroque period helped to bring the anonymous folklore production of the common people to the fore, and with it the vernacular tongue itself.

The process of Slovakization of Catholic literature lasted for more than 150 years; roughly, from the downfall of the Czech Reformation (1621) to the publication of Bernolák's *Dissertatio philologico-critica de Litteris Slavorum* (1787) and *Grammatica Slavica* (1790), two books which marked the first attempt to standardize the Slovak literary language. Historians have supplied many and various explanations for Bernolák's attempt. There is no doubt that Bernolák's Slovak served well the needs of the victorious Counter-Reformation, which could not have hoped to succeed in its apologetic literature with either Latin or Czech. Bernolák had been preceded by the Jesuits of Trnava, who had used the Slovak vernacular in proselytizing. The decline of the Czech literary language during this period helped to stimulate the creation of a separate literary language for the Slovaks. Bernolák's action was in perfect harmony with the general ideas of his time and its tendency to do away with the ever-growing disparity between the language of books and the spoken language of the people, which even then was becoming increasingly aware of its linguistic and racial individuality. For this reason it seems inappropriate to refer to Bernolák's (and subsequently to Štúr's) action as the "Czecho-Slovak literary schism," since the term "schism," with its religious connotation, suggests a deviation from established orthodoxy.

But Bernolák's attempt to introduce a new literary language (based on Western Slovak dialects) was not successful, and failed to win the support of Slovak Protestant writers and scholars. Bernolák even failed to win the support of a large part of the Slovak Catholic clergy, who were already being drawn into the orbit of Magyar culture under the pressure of ecclesiastical and state administrations. In the 1790's the Magyars succeeded in passing legislation favoring the use of the Magyar language throughout Hungary, just as Vienna had made German the privileged language of state in the Austrian half of the Empire. Still, Bernolák's school produced a great, if solitary, poet in the person of Jan Hollý. Bernolák himself founded a number of learned societies devoted to the promotion of Slovak letters; his followers and supporters established several libraries and research centers for ethnographical, historical and philological studies. Following Bernolák's example the Protestants founded several literary societies and a chair of Czechoslovak language and literature at Bratislava, thus indicating that they considered the Czech and

Slovak literary tradition as but one.

But is remained for the younger generation of Slovak Romanticists, mostly of Protestant background, to effect, during
the 1840's, the final separation of Slovak from the Czech literary language, if not from the Czech literary tradition and
cultural life. These young writers, poets and divinity students, led by L'udovít Štur (1815-1856), and strongly influenced by contemporary German philosophy (Herder, Hegel), determined to carry out a separation, not without much hesitation
and fierce struggle with their opponents, led by Jan Kollár, a
prominent Slovak literary and political writer of the older
generation bent on preserving Czech as the sole literary language of the Slovaks.

Contemporary social and political changes, the fierce attempts of the Budapest court to Magyarize the entire country,
together with the tradition of the Enlightenment, with its emphasis on more humane treatment of the common people – all
brought a resolve to preserve and strengthen Slovak national
ideology and the use of the vernacular language. At the same
time a powerful demand for a change in literary style and
taste made itself manifest. The young Romanticists could hardly
be satisfied with the "classicist" works of poets and writers
of the preceding generation. The classicist poets cultivated
"high" forms and lofty themes, out of joint with social and
political conditions and the material and spiritual circum-
stances of the Slovak common people, which (presumably) was
intended to consume this literature. Odes on ancient Greece,
on Homer, Socrates and Virgil were in abundance, as well as
elegies on the Slovak and Slavic past, real, presumed or ima-
ginary. These obsolete themes and forms were rejected by the
Romanticists. Thus in artistic literature itself the premises
existed for rejection both of pseudo-classical literature and
of the language in which it was written. Most of it was in
Czech (Kollár's Slávy dcera) or in Bernolák's Slovak (Hollý's
epics). Hence the Romanticists determined to create a new,
"unspoiled" medium for the expression of their literary, social and political ideas. They were, of course, well aware of
the danger of such a venture. But they realized even better
that it was imperative to rally all Slovaks to the banner of
a uniform language, in view of the rapidly progressing Magyar-
ization of all strata of Slovak society.

Štúr and his followers took upon themselves the grandiose
task of organizing the whole of Slovak national life along the
lines of enlightened humanism. They are to be considered not
only the creators of the standard Slovak literary language,
but as the real founders of Slovak literature proper. In 1845
Štúr founded the first Slovak political newspaper. In 1849 the

Slovak language was recognized as the language of instruction in several secondary schools. But three years later it was relegated to a secondary status, and finally, under the Act of 1907, was almost completely excluded from the schools, public offices and courts of law.

The School of Stur produced a variety of forceful writers and poets, such as Andrej Sladkovič, Janko Kral', Jan Botto and others. Kral', a typical Romanticist in his writings and way of life, is today claimed by Slovak poets as their only true precursor.

While the classicists of the older period had cultivated highly integrated forms, with Romanticism and the new literary language (based on Central Slovak dialects) there appeared syncretized forms. This was in conformity with general Romanticist taste throughout Europe. A combined lyrico-epic genre became dominant. Typical of this tendency during the 1830's and 1840's was the ballad, which often combined the devices of lyric, epic and dramatic poetry. "Low" forms became the favorite of the Romanticists, and with them folklore once again came to the fore of literary interest. It should be noted that this interest in folklore has coincided almost exactly with those periods of Slovak history in which demands for, or defense of, the standardization of Slovak were heard, as in the Baroque period.

For the first time in Slovakia, Štúr's group established a firmly developed code of esthetics for literature. Literary production grew rapidly, both in quantity and quality, and a historian of literature finds it impossible to trace the evolution of Slovak literature chronologically or by generations. Classification, not chronology is important. As in any immature literary structure, a number of divergent literary styles co-existed peacefully in Slovakia until recent times. Criticism was weakly developed, patriotic ardor was high, and every sort of literary production could only be welcomed. Even in Štúr's generation there were writers who may be called classicists in their poetry, though they followed Romanticist esthetics in their dramatic works and a realistic style in their prose. Divergent literary styles co-existed during this so-called "Post-Romantic" period up to the beginnings of literary Realism as a school in the last two decades of the nineteenth century. While this phenomenon has never been satisfactorily explained on a purely literary basis, it may be suggested that the almost total absence of a reading public, combined with a lack of systematic literary criticism, were at least partly responsible.

The process of building a Slovak society, begun so hopefully in 1848, came to an almost catastrophic crisis, during which even some members of Štúr's own generation despaired of the possibility of preserving the Slovak literary language. During the 1880's the Slovaks officially adopted the tactics of political passivity in their struggle with the Magyars. Still, perhaps even because of this, the Slovaks, then a nation without schools, without scientific or cultural institutions, strove ardently to create a full-fledged literature. Ideologically and politically they lagged behind the other European nations during this period, but in literature they kept pace with them. Only thus can one understand the emergence of such prolific writers as Vajanský and Hviezdoslav. Vajanský, almost alone, created the modern Slovak novel. An author of "romans-à-thèse," he is a typical representative of "art for art's sake" in that there is a disparity between his work and the true situation in Slovak society of the day. Both Vajanský and Hviezdoslav strove to elevate the Slovak language to a degree where it would be able to fulfil the highest esthetic functions. Translations from world literature were made during this period (Shakespeare, Goethe, Puškin, Tolstoj, Lermontov, Mickiewicz; later Björnson and Ibsen), and also served to raise the level of the national literature, as well as to demonstrate the expressive possibilities of Slovak.

The works of Hviezdoslav, Vajanský and the prose writer, Martin Kukučin, have often been grouped together in traditional literary history under the single heading of "literary realism," though this term is exact only in its application to Kukučin, a realist who, like the French realists (and the later naturalists) avoided any attempt to evaluate the phenomena of life which he treated.

In classifying Slovak literature of the past eighty years, literary historians have all too often been content with mere chronology, with the grouping of writers by generations, and have avoided the problem of classification. Thus, for example, many prose writers were summarily grouped in the almost meaningless category of "Post-War Literature," simply because they published their work after the first World War. Actually, many of these writers belong, both by the structure of their works and by their generation, to pre-war realism. The sole difference was that before the war realists had cultivated non-historic themes, while after the war most of their subjects were taken from history. Not until the 1930's did Slovak literary realism of the pre-war type cease to dominate Slovak prose, a solitary exception being prose of the so-called expressionistic type.

Modernism and symbolism in Slovak poetry are represented in the work of Ivan Krasko and a few others. In distinction from Hviezdoslav, the Slovak symbolists cultivated the subjective lyric almost completely. Krasko's period (the turn of the century) marks the end of the epic form. And it is likewise significant that Slovak Symbolism created almost no prose. The smaller lyric forms predominated, and free verse was widely cultivated.

The liberation of Slovakia in 1918 brought a tremendous increase both in literary production and the size of the reading public. But this change had no perceptible effect on the existing literary styles (realism in prose, symbolism in poetry), until the 1930's.

During the last fifteen years poetry has regained its former predominance over prose. But the modern lyric, unlike its symbolist predecessor, tends toward a greater objectivity, and again one finds epics and odes. Especially active was the group of surrealists, who described their school as "the historical tail of Romanticism." Like the Romanticists, they sought the congruence of dream, love, life and poetry. Thus modern Slovak literature is closer to Romanticism than to any other period of Slovak literary art.

BIBLIOGRAPHY
SLOVAK LITERATURE AND RELATED FIELDS

See also works marked with an asterisk (*) in the Czech section of the bibliography.

A double asterisk (**) indicates works which also pertain to Czech literature and related fields.

GENERAL WORKS
Historical and Cultural Background

1. Bobek, Wladyslaw, *Slovensko a Slovanstvo*, Bratislava, 1936.

2. Bokes, František, "Dejiny Slovákov a Slovenska," *Slovenská vlastiveda.* Bratislava, 1946, IV, 1-442.

3. Denis, Ernest, *Les Slovaques*, Paris, 1913.

4. Eisner, Jan, "Slovensko v praveku," *Práce Učené společnosti Šafaříkovy*, Vol. XIII, Bratislava, 1933.

5. Hrušovský, František, *Slovenské dejiny*, Turčiansky Sv. Martin, 1939.

**6. Jakobson, Roman, "The Beginnings of National Self-Determination in Europe," *The Review of Politics*, VII, 1 (Jan., 1945), pp. 29-42.

7. Janšák, Štefan, *Slovensko v dobe uhorského feudalismu*, Bratislava, 1932.

8. Krčméry, Štefan, *Prehľad dejín slovenskej literatúry a vzdelanosti*, Turčiansky Sv. Martin, 1920.

9. -----, *Ľudia a knihy*, Prague, 1928.

**10. Locher, Th.J.G., *Die nationale Differenzierung und Integrierung der Slovaken und Tschechen*, Haarlem, 1931.

11. Paulíny, Eugen, "Dejiny spisovnej slovenčiny," *Naučná knižnica*, Vol. XIV, Slovenska akademia vied a umení, Bratislava, 1948.

12. Pražák, Albert "Duchovná podstata slovenskej slovesnosti," *Postavy a dílo*, Prague, Vols. XVIII and XIX, 1933.

13. Škultéty, Jozef, *O Slovákoch*, Turčiansky Sv. Martin, 1928.

14. ------, *Stodvadsaťpäť rokov zo slovenského života (1790-1914)*, Turčiansky Sv. Martin, 1920.

15. Vážný, Václav, "Spisovný jazyk slovenský," *Československá vlastivěda*, Prague, 1936, Second Series, I, 145-215.

16. Vlček, Jaroslav, *Slovensko*, Turčiansky Sv. Martin, 1932.

Surveys of Slovak Literature

17. Bobek, Wladyslaw, *Prehľadné dejiny slovenskej literatúry*, Bratislava, 1939.

**18. Bujnák, Pavel, *Stručné dejiny literatúry československej*, Banská Štiavnica, 1923.

19. Chrobák, Dobroslav, *Rukoväť dejín slovenskej literatúry*, 2nd ed., Prague, 1936.

20. Mráz, Andrej, "Dejiny slovenskej literatúry," *Vlastivedná knižnica Slovenskej akademie vied a umení*, Bratislava, 1948, XIV, 1-328.

21. ------, *Die Literatur der Slovaken*, Berlin, Prague, Vienna, 1942.

22. Krčméry, Štefan, "A Survey of Modern Slovak Literature," *Slavonic and East European Review*, VI, 19 (June, 1928), pp. 160-170.

23. ------, *Stopäťdesiat rokov slovenskej literatúry*, I-II, Turčiansky Sv. Martin, 1943.

24. ------, "Úvod do dejín slovenskej literatúry, najmä poézie," *Sborník Matice slovenskej*, Vol. XVIII, Turčiansky Sv. Martin, 1943.

25. Pražák, Albert, "Literatura slovenská," *Československá vlastivěda*, Prague, 1933, VII, 209-272.

26. Vlček, Jaroslav, *Dejiny literatúry slovenskej*, Turčiansky Sv. Martin, 1890, 1923, 1933.

27. ------, "K dejinám literatúry slovenskej," *Slovenské pohľady*, Vol. XVIII, 1898.

28. ------, *Literatura na Slovensku; její vznik, rozvoj, význam a úspěchy*, Prague, 1881.

29. Bakoš, Mikuláš, *Problém vývinovej periodizácie slovenskej literatúry*, Trnava, 1942.

30. -----, *Vývin slovenského verša*, Turčiansky Sv. Martin, 1939.

31. Bobek, Wladyslaw, "Mickiewicz v literaturze slowackej," *Práce Učené společnosti Šafaříkovy*, Bratislava, 1931, IV, 1-61.

32. Bujnák, Pavel, *Dve kapitoly z literárnej estetiky*, Prešov, 1927.

33. -----, "Hlavné prúdy a smery v slovenskej literatúre," *Slovenská čítanka*, 2nd. ed., Brno, 1925.

34. Hofman, J., *Staré umenie na Slovensku*, Prague, 1930.

35. Mocko, J., *Historia posvätnej piesne slovenskej a historia kancionálu*, I-II, Liptovský Sv. Mikuláš, 1909-12.

36. Wagner, Vladimír, *Dejiny výtvarného umenia na Slovensku*, Trnava, 1930.

OLD CHURCH SLAVONIC PERIOD

**37. Dvorník, František, *Les Légendes de Constantine et de Méthode vues de Byzance*, Prague, 1933.

**38. -----, *Les Slaves, Byzance et Rome au IXe siècle*, Paris, 1926.

**39. Holinka, Rudolf, *Začiatky vzdelanosti vo Veľkomoravskej ríši*, Turčiansky Sv. Martin, 1949. (Reprinted from *Jazykovedný sborník Matice slovenskej*, Vol. II, 1949).

**40. Stanislav, Ján, ed., "Ríša Veľkomoravská," *Osvetová knižnica*, Vol. III, Mazáč and Prague.

41. -----, *Kultúra starých Slovákov*, Bratislava, 1944.

**42. -----, *Slovanskí apoštoli Cyril a Metod a ich činnosť vo Veľkomoravskej ríši*, Bratislava, 1944.

RENAISSANCE AND BAROQUE,
REFORMATION AND COUNTER-REFORMATION (TO 1790)

43. Bálent, B.C., *Bardejovské katechizmy z rokov 1581-1612*, Turčiansky Sv. Martin, 1947.

44. Banik, A.A., *Ján Baltazár Magin a jeho politická, národná i kultúrna obrana Slovákov r. 1728*, Trnava, 1936.

45. -----, *Novšie údaje na poznanie Jána Baltazára Magina, jeho diela i doby*, Trnava, 1937.

46. Brtáň, Rudolf, *Barokový slavizmus*, Liptovský Sv. Mikuláš, 1939.

47. -----, *Danielovo Sinapiovo Horčičkovo Neo-Forum Latino-Slavonicum*, Liptovský Sv. Mikuláš, 1940.

48. Bucko, V., *Mikuláš Oláh a jeho doba (1493-1568)*, Bratislava, 1940.

49. Ďurovič, Ján, *Duchovná poézia slovenská pred Tranovským*, Liptovský Sv. Mikuláš, 1939.

50. -----, *Evanjelická literatúra do tolerancie*, Turčiansky Sv. Martin, 1940.

51. Gajdoš, V.J., *Život a dielo Jána Abrahamffyho*, Turčiansky Sv. Martin, 1942.

52. Chaloupecký, Václav, "Universita Petra Pázmánya a Slovensko (1635-1935)," *Sborníky Učené společnosti Šafaříkovy*, Bratislava, 1935.

53. Krčméry, Štefan, "Slovenská poézia 16. storočia," *Sborník Matice slovenskej*, Vol. X, Turčiansky Sv.Martin, 1932.

54. Kvačala, Ján, *Dejiny reformácie na Slovensku (1517-1711)*, Liptovský Sv. Mikuláš, 1935.

55. Mišík, M., *Husiti na Slovensku*, Banská Bystrica, 1927.

56. Mráz, Andrej, *Gavlovičova škola kresťanská*, Bratislava, 1940.

57. Oberuč, J., *Črty zo života a diela Mateja Bela*, Bratislava, 1940.

58. Osuský, Samuel Št., ed., *Tranovského sborník*, Liptovský Sv. Mikuláš, 1936.

59. Pöstényi, Ján, *Slovenský národný život v Trnave v rokoch 1488-1820.* Trnava, 1943.

60. Stanislav, Ján, "Slovenský juh v stredoveku," *Spisy Jazykovedného odboru Matice slovenskej,* Series B, Vols. I-II, Turčiansky Sv. Martin, 1948.

61. Učená spoločnost Šafaříkova, *Sborník k 300. výročí kancionálu Cithara Sanctorum,* Bratislava, 1936. (Reprinted from *Bratislava,* X, 1-2).

62. Varsik, Branko, *Husiti a reformácia na Slovensku do žilinskej synody,* Bratislava, 1932.

63. -----, *Národnostný problém trnavskej univerzity,* Bratislava, 1938.

THE PERIOD OF ENLIGHTENMENT
AND THE BEGINNINGS OF
THE STANDARDIZED SLOVAK LITERARY LANGUAGE

64. Čapek, Jan Blahoslav, *Augustin Doležal a jeho Tragoedia,* Bratislava, 1931.

65. Hirner, Alexander, *Ján Feješ, jeho dielo a myšlienková sústava,* Turčiansky Sv. Martin, 1942.

66. Jankovič, V., *Ján Čaplovič; život, osobnosť a dielo,* Turčiansky Sv. Martin, 1945.

67. Lepáček, Cyril, *Vojtech Šimko, spisovateľ Bernolákovej školy,* Turciansky Sv. Martin, 1942.

68. Pražák, Albert, *Dějiny spisovné slovenštiny po dobu Štúrovu,* Prague, 1928.

69. Rapant, Daniel, *K počiatkom maďarizácie,* I-II, Bratislava, 1927-31.

70. -----, *Maďarónstvo Bernolákovo,* Bratislava, 1930.

71. Stanislav, Ján, *K jazykovednému dielu Antona Bernoláka,* Bratislava, 1941.

72. Vilikovský, Jan, *Dějiny literárních společností malohontských,* Bratislava, 1935.

73. Vlček, Jaroslav, "Bernolák a jeho doba," *Slovenské pohľady*, Vol. X, 1890.

74. Zlatoš, Štefan, *Písmo sväté u bernolákovcov (Juraj Palkovič a jeho slovenský preklad Biblie)*, Trnava, 1939.

FROM CLASSICISM TO ROMANTICISM;
THE FINAL CODIFICATION OF STANDARD SLOVAK

75. Goláň, Karol, *Rok so štúrovcami*, Myjava, 1945.

**76. Hodža, Milan, *Československý rozkol*, Turčiansky Sv. Martin, 1920.

77. Pražák, Albert, "The Slavonic Congress of 1848 and the Slovaks," *Slavonic and East European Review*, VII, 19 (June, 1928), pp. 141–159.

78. -----, "The Slovak Sources of Kollár's Pan-Slavism," *Slavonic Review*, VI, 18 (March, 1928), pp. 579–592.

79. Rapant, Daniel, *Slovenské povstanie roku 1848-1849*, I-II, Turčiansky Sv. Martin, 1937.

80. Tourtzer (Turcerová), Hélène, *Louis Stúr et l'idée de l'indépendence slovaque (1815-1856)*, Paris, 1913.

81. Bujnák, Pavel, *Dr. Karol Kuzmány*, Liptovský Sv.Mikuláš, 1927.

82. Hurban, Jozef Miloslav, *Ľudovít Štúr*, I-III, Turčiansky Sv. Martin, 1928-42.

83. Pišút, Milan, *K počiatkom básnickej školy Štúrovej*, Bratislava, 1938.

84. Vlček, Jaroslav, "Štúrova škola na Slovensku," *Literatura česká XIX. století*, Prague, 1907, Vol. III, Part I, pp. 401-445.

Specialized Questions

85. Čiževský, Dmitrij, *Štúrova filosofie života*, Bratislava, 1941.

86. Osuský, Samuel Št., *Filozofia štúrovcov*, I-II, Myjava, 1926-28.

87. Pallová, V., *Antika v literárnych teóriach Jonáša Zábor-ského*, Trnava, 1944.

88. Pražák, Albert, "Hegen bei den Slovaken," *Hegen bei den Slaven*, ed. *D.Čyževskij, Veröffentlichungen der Slavistischen Arbeitsgemeinschaft an der Deutschen Universität in Prag*, Reichenberg-Liberec, 1934, Series I, Vol. IX, pp. 397-429.

89. Rampák, Zoltán, *K charakteru štúrovskej drámy*, Turčiansky Sv. Martin, 1947.

90. Šimončič, Klement, "K.H.Mácha a Slovensko," *Slovenské pohľady*, LII, 8-9 (August-September, 1936), pp. 443-452.

POST-ROMANTICISM, REALISM AND MODERNISM
IN SLOVAK POETRY
(From the 1860's to World War I)

91. Mráz, Andrej, "Matica slovenská v rokoch 1863-1875," *Ľudová knižnica Matice slovenskej*, Vol. I, Turčiansky Sv. Martin, 1935.

92. Ormis, Ján V., *Zo slovenskej minulosti národnej a literár-nej*, Prague, 1932.

93. Pöstényi, Ján, *Dejiny Spolku sv. Vojtecha*, Trnava, 1929.

94. Vlček, Jaroslav, *Slovensko od reakce Bachovy do zrušení Matice slovenské (1850-1875)*, Prague, 1913.

Literature of the Period (1860-1918)

95. Brezina, Ján, *Ivan Krasko*, Bratislava, 1946.

96. Bujnák, Pavel, *Hviezdoslav*, Bratislava, 1919.

97. Kostolný, Andrej, *O Hviezdoslavovej tvorbe*, Bratislava, 1939.

98. Matuška, Alexander, *Vajanský prozaik*, Bratislava, 1946.

99. Mráz, Andrej, *Andrej Sytniansky v slovenskej literatúre sedemdesiatich rokov XIX. storočia*, Turčiansky Sv. Martin, 1945.

100. ————, *Ján Kalinčiak*, Turčiansky Sv. Martin, 1936.

101. Pražák, Albert, *Literární Slovensko let padesátých až sedmdesátých*, Prague, 1932.

102. ————, *Studentská léta Svetozara Hurbana Vajanského*, Bratislava, 1925.

103. Sedlák, Ján, *Literárne dielo Tichomíra Milkina*, Trnava, 1941.

104. Šteller, F., *Andrej Radlinský*, Trnava, 1934.

CONTEMPORARY SLOVAK LITERATURE
(AFTER THE FIRST WORLD WAR)

105. Medvecký, K.A., *Slovenský prevrat*, I-IV, Trnava, 1930-31.

106. Šrobár, Vavro, *Osvobodené Slovensko*, Vol. I, Prague, 1928.

Literature of the Period (after 1918)

107. Bakoš, Nikolaj, "K vývinu a situácii slovenskej literatúry," *Slovenské smery*, V, 6-8 (May-July, 1938), pp. 250-262.

108. Bor, Ján E., *Poézia povojnového Slovenska*, Trnava, 1934.

109. Bittner, Konrad, *Das Slovakische Schriftum der Nachkriegszeit*, Munich, 1939.

110. Hemaliar, Ján, *Hlasy nášho východu*, Prague, 1929.

111. Jesenský, Ján and Emil B. Lukáč, eds., "Z príležitosti kongresu slovenských spisovateľov v Trenčianskych Tepliciach 30.-31. mája a 1. júna 1936," *Slovenské smery*, III, 8-9 (May-June, 1936), pp. 281-402.

112. ————, eds., "Rokovanie kongresu slovenských spisovateľov v Trenčianskych Tepliciach 30.- 31. mája a 1. júna 1936," *Slovenské smery*, III, 10 (July, 1936), pp. 443-552.

113. Lukáč, Emil Boleslav, ed., *Slovenská tvorba slovesná*, Bratislava, 1936.

114. Považan, Michal, "Vývinové zaradenie nadrealistickej poézie," *Pozdrav*, ed. M.Považan, Bratislava, 1942, pp. 78-90.

115. Smrek, Ján, ed., *Slovenská literárna a umelecká prítomnosť*, Prague, 1931.

116. Zvěřina, L.N., ed., *Slovenská literatura popřevratová*, Prague, 1932. (Anthology).

SELECTED LIST OF SLOVAK PERIODICALS
DEALING WITH
LITERARY SCIENCE AND CRITICISM

Slovenské pohľady; Matica slovenská, Turčiansky Sv. Martin, Vols. I- (1881-).

Slovenská reč, Matica slovenská, Turčiansky Sv. Martin, Vols. I- (1932-).

Elán, Prague, Vols. I-XV (1930-46).

Slovenské smery umelecké a kritické, Prague, Vols. I-II (1933-35); Bratislava, Vols. III-IV(1935-38).

Kultúrny život, Bratislava, Vol. I- (1946-).

LUSATIAN LITERATURE

by

Clarence A. Manning

LUSATIAN LITERATURE

The Lusatians, also called Lusatian Serbs, Sorbs, and Wends, form the smallest existing Slavic group. They are the last survivors of the Slavs who, in historic times, inhabited Germany as far to the west as the Elbe River. They are now confined in a restricted area extending from the Spreewald near Berlin into Saxony nearly to the Czech border and number in the neighborhood of 120,000. Even among this small group there are two marked subdivisions, for the Lower Lusatians in the north, with their centre at Cottbus (Khoćebuz), speak a dialect closer to Polish, while the Upper Lusatians in the neighborhood of Bautzen (Budyšín) are closer to the Czechs. Lusatian culture has developed under definite Czech influence, and indeed it was the medieval connections between Lusatia and the Kingdom of Bohemia that strengthened the national will to survival.

The Lusatian language was apparently first reduced to writing at the time of the Reformation in the sixteenth century and, curiously enough, the earliest printed books, the Hymnal of Moller and a translation of Luther's Catechism (1574), were in Lower Lusatian, although they were printed in Budyšín. It was not until after the Thirty Years' War that Michael Frencel (Brancel) (1628-1706) printed the first translation of the Gospel in Upper Lusatian. It is also interesting to note that this same man presented an appeal to Peter the Great in the name of Slavdom, when the Tsar visited Germany.

To add to the disunity, the Protestants adopted the German system of orthography, while the Roman Catholics followed the Czech system and thus created new difficulties which continued until the nineteenth century. The language was fostered by the Catholic Lusatian Seminary in Prague, founded in 1706, and the Evangelical Serb Preaching Society established in Leipzig in 1716. The works produced by both groups were largely of a religious character and neither was interested in creating a modern literature. The first serious philological study was made by Jurij Körner (1718-1772) who published in Leipzig in 1766 his *Philologisch-kritische Abhandlung von der Wendischen Sprache und ihrem Nutzen in den Wissenschaften*, written under the influence of the Enlightenment.

The first poet in the modern sense was Jurij Mjen (Möhn) (1729-1785), who followed the antiquated German fashion of poetry and translated parts of Klopstock's *Messiah*. But his works aroused little enthusiasm.

The studies of the Czech scholar Josef Dobrovský brought the Lusatians to the attention of the progressive intellectual circles of Prague and the representatives of the Romantic movement there who gladly included the Lusatians among the various Slav peoples. Their literature and folksongs were treated by P. J. Šafařík in his *Geschichte der slawischen Sprachen und Literatur* (1826), and his example has been followed by a large number of Czechs, such as Adolf Černý, Jan Máchal, etc.

From the time of Šafařík, a steadily increasing number of scholars have taken an active interest in Lusatian. Among these Izmail Ivanovich Sreznevski based his work on studies among the people. Pypin included them in his *History of Slav Literatures* and so did Talvj; and various Polish scholars have interested themselves in the subject. In recent years, Professor Josef Páta of the Charles University was their most ardent partisan, and his volumes are the most complete and detailed on almost all phases of Lusatian literature and culture.

Early in the nineteenth century, the Lusatians began their modern literature. Handrij Zejleŕ (1804-1872), under the influence of Kollár, commenced to write and was the true founder of the modern literature. He was followed by a group including Jan Arnošt Smoleŕ (1816-1864) and Michael Hórnik (1833-1894). In 1847 there was founded at Budyšín on the Czech pattern the Maćica Serbska, and a delegate from this took part in the Slav Congress in Prague in 1848.

The next generation of the Young Lusatians under the leadership of the leading poet Jakub Bart-Cišinski (1856-1909) and the philologist Arnošt Muka (1854-1932) followed closely the development among the Czechs and based their theories on the works of the Czech authors of the period. They were followed by a younger group such as Miklawš Andricki (1871-1908), who were largely under the influence of Thomas G. Masaryk. Many had been his students at the Charles University, and they gave to the growing literature the stamp of his personality and ideas.

By 1918 the Lusatians ventured to hope for some recognition of their national identity by the Congress of Versailles, but they were sadly disappointed and their leaders who attended the conference were later arrested by the German Republic and sentenced to long terms in prison. This did not break up the movement, and a new generation of authors of whom we may cite Józef Nowak (b. 1895), Jan Skala (b. 1882) and Mina Witkojc

(b. 1893), a Lower Lusatian, continued to develop the literature in accordance with the post-war ideals of Czechoslovakia.

This flourishing movement came to an end with the accession to power of Adolph Hitler in 1933. The Maćica Serbska was closed and most of its publications were stopped. The repression of the movement became ever more severe until World War II. Since that time the Lusatians have been behind the iron curtain and subjected only to the influences of modern Communism.

The entire Lusatian revival is the story of the struggle of a small people, against overwhelming odds, to resist the impact of Germanism and to adapt themselves to the modern world. Despite their love of the theatre, the Lusatians were never able to develop more than groups of talented amateurs; they were able to support only one daily newspaper; they had no control over their school system, which was in German hands, and they had no representative in the German Reichstag, owing to the political division of their lands between Prussia and Saxony. Yet, despite all these handicaps, they succeeded by their own efforts in breathing new life into the Lusatian communities and they produced a small but excellent literature which cannot be neglected in any review of the Slavic achievements of the last century and a half.

BIBLIOGRAPHY
LUSATIAN LITERATURE

1. Kuba, Ludwik, *Čtení o Lužici*, Prague, 1925.

2. Máchal, Jan, *Slovanské literatury*, Prague, 1922-29.

3. Manning, Clarence A., "Lusatian Literature," *A Handbook of of Slavic Studies*, ed. L.I.Strakhovsky, Cambridge, Mass., 1949, pp. 532-534.

4. Páta, Josef, *Srbská čítanka*, Prague, 1920.

5. -----, *Úvod do studia lužickosrbského písemnictví*, Prague, 1925. Lusatian edition, Budyšín, 1929.

6. -----, *Z kulturního života lužických Srbů po světové válce*, Prague, 1929. Lusatian edition, Budyšín, 1932.

7. -----, *Les Serbes de Lusace: littérature et culture après la grande guerre*, Paris, 1934.

8. -----, *Lužické stati*, Prague, 1937.

9. Phaliapau, Marie, *La littérature des Serbes de Lusace*, Paris, 1928.

10. Pypin, A.N., *Istorija slavjanskikh literatur*, St.Petersburg, 1879-81.

Bei Fragen zur Produktsicherheit wenden Sie sich bitte an:
If you have any questions regarding product safety,
please contact:

Walter de Gruyter GmbH
Genthiner Straße 13
10785 Berlin
productsafety@degruyterbrill.com